STARS OF THE NBA

17
CELTICS
11

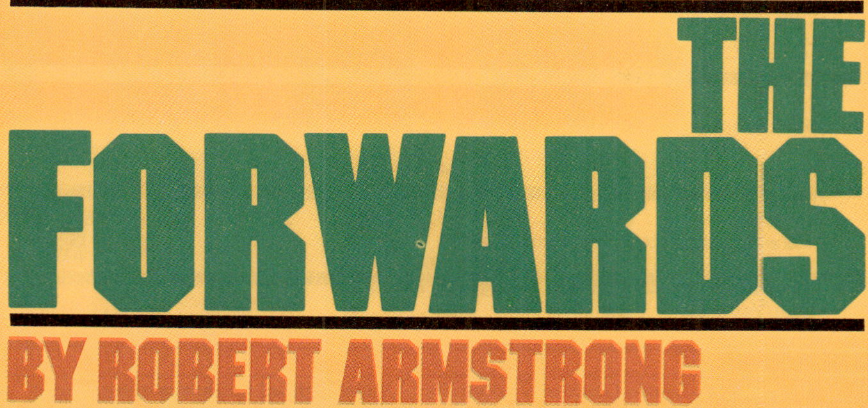

CREATIVE EDUCATION / CHILDRENS PRESS

RICK BARRY

Rick Barry, the vagabond of pro basketball, finally found a home and some measure of contentment in 1975. The rest of the National Basketball Association (NBA) was not very happy about that because it could mean only trouble.

While Barry was bouncing from team to team and league to league early in his career, he was one of the better forwards in the game. Now that he has settled with the Golden State Warriors, he is the best.

Barry, 6 feet, 7½-inches and 220 pounds, has the ideal size for the position he plays. He has always had the gaudy statistics that distinguish premier players in any sport. Then in the 1974-1975 season he led a team of unknown players to the NBA title, fulfilling a long-held ambition.

He led with his skills and in his role as team captain, a position he had never held before at any level. Rarely has any player been able to lead by example as well as he did.

Warriors

24

Ray Scott, then the coach of the Detroit Pistons, has pinpointed the difference in Barry. Scott noted that the Warriors had gotten rid of Nate Thurmond, Cazzie Russell, Clyde Lee, and Jim Barnett to field a much younger team. Scott said, "Basketball is a game of ego. Subtract four egos from five and what you have left is a man who knows where he is going."

"Before he had too many egos to think about. They tell me it (being captain) means a lot to Rick and I believe it because he plays like it does. Right now he is playing as well as anyone who has ever played this game."

Al Attles, the Warriors' coach who sought the changes Scott mentioned, agreed. "Captain, well, that's never been a big deal," Attles once commented. "I mean, what does the captain do? Shake hands at the centerline before the game starts? But Rick brought a new dimension to it."

The change led to the kind of season most players dream about. Barry terrorized the opposition in every phase of the game in 1974-1975. He was second in the league in scoring with a 30.6 per game average, tops in foul shooting and steals, and sixth in assists — passes that lead directly to baskets by teammates. All the other top 10 assist leaders were guards.

Barry's performance in the 17 play-off games the Warriors needed to win the 1975 NBA title was just as impressive. He scored 479 points (a 28.1 average), had 103 assists, pulled down 94 rebounds, and made 50 steals, eight in one game. The latter two figures were each league records.

Barry was named the most valuable player in the play-offs. Tom Heinsohn, the coach of the Boston Celtics, the team the Warriors replaced as champions, went a step further. He called Barry "the best all-around player in the game."

Playing forward in professional basketball is the best way to sample all phases of the game. Once upon a time, teams merely picked the two tallest players other than the center, stationed them in the corners, and had them shoot over the opposition. Their only other job was to get as many rebounds as possible.

Then came the idea of teaming players with complimentary skills, pairing, for example, a "quick" forward with a "power" forward. The quick forward could drive to the basket for a layup as well as shoot over his opponent. The power forward could rebound with taller centers and start fast breaks.

Today a well-rounded forward participates in all phases of the game. He must shoot, pass, rebound, set picks, move without the ball, defend, and run on the fast break.

Guards, on the other hand, often need not rebound and centers do not necessarily have to pass well or run on the fast break.

The best players at each position can do those things, but the forward in pro basketball must do them.

The stars naturally can do more of those things well. For example, George McGinnis, though considered a power forward, is quick enough to play even at guard.

Though lacking weight and muscle, Julius Erving can jump well enough to match rebounds with centers.

Rick Barry and John Havlicek, because of their experience and knowledge, can fill either role and David Thompson, thoúgh physically outsized, makes up for his size with his phenomenal quickness and jumping ability.

To be considered, then, one of the best at the forward position is one of the highest compliments in basketball.

Barry's ability to play was never in question, but his life as a pro basketball player was not always so rosy, and Rick had often been his own worst enemy. He was drafted out of the University of Miami in Florida by the Warriors following the 1964-1965 college season during which he led the nation in scoring. He won the NBA rookie of the year award by averaging 25.7 points per game in his first season. But soon his life on the treadmill started.

After another bright season with the Warriors he became the first NBA star to jump leagues, joining Oakland of the since disbanded American Basketball Association (ABA). The Warriors sued, the first of many legal problems for Barry during the next five years, and Barry was forced to sit out a season.

Then it became one city after another — Oakland (ABA), Washington (ABA), and New York (ABA) — before a judge halted the roadshow and sent Rick back to the Warriors following the 1972 season.

24
BUCKS
ASSOCIATION

24
Bucks
21

On his tour of cities, however, Rick had been busy. Not only had he become the first player to have been the top scorer in the NBA and the ABA; he had also acquired a reputation as a hothead, a man who could not control his temper. He would scream at officials and fight with opposing players over the slightest wrong.

He also suffered two serious knee injuries and acquired the tag of a greedy gypsy who would play for whichever team offered the most money.

It was a reputation Rick didn't like. "I think it's unfair," Rick once said. "I'm supposed to be money-hungry, but I always played with the team with which I had a contract or I sat out."

Rich has said his reputation as a hothead is also undeserved and there are those who agree with him. Many observers feel he is manhandled more without fouls being called than any other non-center in the NBA.

Both his fights with opposing players and his explosions at referees are usually provoked by his aggressive play, his opponents' attempts to stop him, and the referees' failure to blow their whistles.

"My game is to drive to the hoop and try to draw a foul," Rick has observed. "When I feel the initial contact, I start to twist and turn to get the shot off. What happens is that the refs sometimes lose sight of the body contact because they follow the flight of the ball. The only thing that really gets my goat is when an opposing player gets upset when he's caught for butchering me and then acts as if he never touched me."

In the drive to the Warriors 1975 championship, however, Rick matured. He did not draw a technical foul during the play-offs. "It took me 10 years to realize you can't win an argument with an official." he says.

In a volatile matchup with Mike Riordan of Baltimore during the finals, Rick calmly walked away when the frustrated Riordan tried to pick a fight. "I amazed myself at my restraint," Rick said then.

That restraint was a long time in coming. Even in college, Bruce Hale, his coach at Miami and later at Oakland, warned him of the need for it. Hale has said, "What I tried to teach Rick was how to behave on the court. The image you develop on the court will stay with you later on."

Hale was not only Rick's coach, he is his father-in-law. Rick is married to Hale's daughter, Pam.

The image Rick presents now is that of a perfectionist. He credits that to his father, his first coach and teacher when he was growing up in New Jersey.

"My father was a strict fundamentalist and disciplinarian," Rick once recalled. "He made sure I knew how to dribble without looking at the ball, how to pass, and how to run backwards.

"Take the way I shoot free throws. He taught me to shoot them underhand. To this day I think I'm a better free throw shooter because I shoot underhand." Barry is the only NBA player who shoots free throws this way and he also makes more of them than any other player.

Rick considered retirement at the age of 31 after fulfilling his ambition of winning a NBA championship. He wanted to become a sportscaster, but he couldn't get the deal he wanted from a national network. That didn't leave him without any goals as he continued to lead the Warriors.

"You know what I want now," he told reporters, "what I dream about? It's playing the perfect game . . . shutting my man off with nothing . . . not missing a single shot or a single free throw . . . not making a single turnover . . . the perfect game."

That's impossible, of course, but if anyone was capable of doing it, it would be Rick Barry.

GOLDEN STATE
24
WARRIORS

Call him Dr. J or, simply, The Doctor. It is the best name in sports in years and years and even basketball fans who have never seen him play know that it belongs to Julius Erving, the most exciting player in the game.

Dr. J not only excites fans; he excites pro basketball owners. When he had a chance to bid for Julius' services in October 1976, F. Eugene Dixon, the millionaire owner of the Philadelphia 76ers, got excited enough to reportedly spend $6 million.

When the NBA's first 1976-1977 regular season game was played, Dr. J had not reported to the New York Nets, one of four teams from the disbanded ABA taken into the NBA in June 1976. Dr. J and the Nets were in a salary hassle. Dr. J wanted to renegotiate the remaining four years on a reported seven-year, $1.9 million contract.

NETS
32
24
21

People in the NBA wanted Dr. J playing for someone. He was the major attraction to the NBA in adding the Nets and teams from Denver, Indiana and San Antonio to the 18 existent NBA teams. The Nets finally permitted some other teams to deal with Erving.

Dr. J ended up in a 76ers uniform in time for that team's first game of the season. The 26-year-old superstar and the 76ers reportedly agreed to a multi-year contract said to pay Julius some $600,000, which amount is reported to be the most ever paid a basketball player. The Nets were reportedly to receive $3 million for Julius' contract from the 76ers, who were said to have five other players whose contracts called for $1 million or more in bonus and salaries.

Knowledgeable basketball people knew Erving was going to be good when he left college. He left the University of Massachusetts after his junior year to join the Virginia Squires. He came to the pros through the so-called "hardship draft," a ploy pro basketball owners established to take players still in college. Until the "hardship draft" was developed, the pros said a player's class had to graduate before he could be drafted.

"Good" does not quite describe the way he entered the league in 1971. He averaged 27.3 points per game in his rookie year and followed that with a 31.9 average for the 1972-1973 season. Spectacular! Then, when he was considering joining the NBA, the Squires traded him to the Nets in order to keep him from jumping to the other league.

The Nets were able to pay Julius the multi-million dollar contract he wanted and the move enabled him to play close to home. Changing uniforms and teammates did not slow Julius down a bit.

In the 1974-1975 season, for example, Julius, a fourth-year pro, was second in the league in scoring (27.9 average), ranked eighth in rebounding (10.8), seventh in assists (5.5), fourth in blocked shots (1.8), tied for third in steals (2.2), and shared the Most Valuable Player award with George McGinnis, then with Indiana.

Erving accomplished all that by having games like this: Against San Diego, while playing only 36 of the 48-minute contest, he sank 19 of 23 shots from the floor, seven of them dunks, made 13 of 15 free throws and finished with 51 points. He also pulled down 19 rebounds. That came on Feb. 22, 1975, Erving's 25th birthday. San Diego wished he had celebrated elsewhere.

It prompted San Diego coach Beryl Shipley to comment, "He's the finest. There's no part of the game he can't do. He can make so many things happen. The stat sheet doesn't say how many times he kept the ball alive off the boards before one of his teammates grabbed the ball or how many times he got his hand on a ball and knocked it loose for someone else to steal."

Adolph Rupp, the legendary retired University of Kentucky coach, once watched the Doctor beat the Kentucky Colonels twice in a row with last second shots and raved about Erving's play. "Right now," Rupp then said, "Julius Erving is the best."

"He's a young man with supreme confidence. Some of the best players I've ever had didn't want to take the last shot," Rupp said. "He's a Babe Ruth. Ruth pointed out to the stands where he was going to hit a home run, and he hit it there. Julius is the same way. Everyone knows he's going to take the last shot (in a close game), and he still makes them. He wants to do it because he knows he can do it."

Julius proved he could do it again in the 1975-1976 season. He again won the Most Valuable Player award, this time by himself, and won his third scoring title in four years with a 29.3 average. The rest of his game was just as brilliant as always. He was fifth best in rebounding, seventh in assists and blocked shots, third in steals, eighth in shooting percentage.

But mere words of praise and the evidence of statistics do not tell why Julius Erving is so exciting. For it is not so much what Erving does as the way that he does it.

Basketball crowds are excited most by the game's leapers and Julius is one of the greatest leapers the game has ever known. There are times he almost seems to defy gravity as he floats through the air toward the basket, deciding what to do with the ball. His huge hands and tremendous body control make a play that is impossible for others appear easy for him.

He can take off from the foul line, the ball resembling a cantaloupe in one hand, the play finishing with a slam dunk that leaves the backboard quivering. Or he may slide along the baseline, take a pass, float up under the basket and beyond, finishing with a two-handed, over-the-head, backhand stuff.

They are moves perfected in the pros but learned on the playgrounds. Julius was born in 1950 in Roosevelt, N.Y., barely a stone's throw from the Nassau Coliseum where the Nets play their home games. His love affair with the game began when most children are still playing hide 'n seek and he credits much of his success to Don Ryan, the coach of a Salvation Army team which Julius played for when he was 10 years old.

NETS
32
WISE
42

"He was very helpful to me in my view of life," Erving once commented about Ryan. "You see, I grew up never knowing I was on the other side of the tracks. Then when I started to look around me and see the way other people were living, I said to Don, 'What do I have to do to get like them?' And he told me, 'You have to perform in school the same as you do on the basketball court.' Unfortunately, a lot of people I played with, excellent ballplayers, just couldn't do it. I did.

"You know, I went to the University of Massachusetts. They are very selective about who they let in there. That is no jocks' school."

But Don Ryan does not like to take so much credit. "His mother is the reason," Ryan has said. "She washed floors and the kid copied her. He was out delivering morning newspapers from four until eight every morning. He got it all from her."

Whatever the reason, while some of his friends were often in trouble, Julius was never a problem, possibly because playground basketball took so much of his time.

"I was only 6-feet, 3-inches when I graduated from high school," Julius once noted, (he's grown to 6-6 and weighs 200 pounds). "Yet I always had big hands and could jump (he could dunk in the 7th grade), so I learned to be trickier than bigger guys.

"I like to experiment. I loved to watch guys and what they'd do in emergency situations. When I practiced, I worked on ways to take advantage of my advantages. I set no dimensions for my game; I decided not to limit myself.

"I've said many times that an athlete should dare to be great . . . should dare to be different, to try to see if he can do it better than the next guy. See if he can do something he can't possibly do. That's the challenge; that's the fun of it."

Kevin Loughery, the Nets coach who played in the NBA through the 1960's, had always considered Elgin Baylor, the former Los Angeles Laker star, the best forward he had ever seen.

That was before Julius came along.

Now, Loughery told newsmen, "When it comes to the over-all game, the defensive end as well as the offensive, Doc is better than Elgin. He plays his best against good teams and in front of big crowds. He accepts a challenge. He responds to the crowd and the importance of the game. All the great ones do."

DAVID THOMPSON

David Thompson is the "Boy Wonder" of professional basketball. In 1975-1976, his rookie season with the Denver Nuggets, he averaged an even 26 points per game, third highest in the American Basketball Association, a league in its final season of existence.

He was also among the league leaders in steals and was one of his team's best shot blockers and most accurate shooters.

Other players down through the years have turned the basketball world on its ear with impressive rookie seasons. Kareem Abdul-Jabbar, Dave Cowens, Wilt Chamberlain, Artis Gilmore, Spencer Haywood, and Wes Unseld all compiled impressive first-year statistics while winning rookie of the year honors.

But those men are all 6-feet, 8-inches or taller. David Thompson is 6-feet, 3½-inches, and no one his size has ever started his pro career the way he has.

Denver
33

ERVING
32

But the way David began came as no surprise. After watching him play three years at North Carolina State, there was not a doubt in anyone's mind about him. During his junior year in college, pro scouts were already saying that he was "a player who comes along maybe once every 10 or 20 years."

Fred Schaus, now the coach at Purdue was one of the first to recognize David's talents. While Schaus was still general manager of the Los Angeles Lakers, he said of David, "Thompson is better right now than Jerry West when he was a senior. He is one of the best players in the country today, pros included."

That was said before David had ever played a varsity game for North Carolina State and after he had led all freshman scorers in the country with a 38.6 average.

There were few men around willing to argue with Schaus after Thompson's final game as a collegian. The North Carolina native had been named to the All-American team in each of his three varsity seasons.

As a junior he had been the key figure in halting UCLA's national college championship string at seven. Thompson led State over UCLA and Bill Walton in the 1974 semifinals. The double-overtime game was one of the most thrilling on record. State then went on to defeat Marquette, 76-64, for the 1974 NCAA title.

Though State did not repeat as champions in David's senior year, he led the Wolfpack to a 22-6 record, averaging 29.9 points per game to finish as the nation's third highest scorer.

All of this was accomplished with a flair and style that left basketball fans everywhere breathless and North Carolina State fans ecstatic. Thompson's jumping ability was already a legend. It was said he had a vertical jump of 42 inches, meaning that he could stand under the basket and, leaping straight up, come within 2½ inches of hitting his head on the rim.

And it was a leaping David Thompson that everyone came to see. Once in the air he seemed to hang suspended; defenders who rose with him quickly fell back as Thompson seemed to soar even higher before deciding what to do with the ball. Though the dunk was then outlawed in college play, Thompson invented a play just as spectacular — the "Alley-oop."

It worked like this: David's teammate Monty Towe, one of the smallest players in the game at 5-5, would loft a high, soft lob toward the backboard. David, breaking toward the basket along the baseline, would leap high above the basket, catch the ball and gently drop it through the hoop. The play was almost unstoppable.

After David once had scored 40 points against Georgia Southern, several on the "Alley-oop," Southern Coach J. E. Rowe shook his head and marveled. "If I hadn't seen it with my own eyes there is no way I'd believe his talents," the coach said. "I'd pay myself to see him play."

Tom Roy, a 6-foot, 9-inch forward from Maryland, once described the trouble he and everyone else had trying to defend against David in college. "There was nothing I could do," Roy said. "We wanted him to shoot from the outside, but he made those; and when I gave him a little room, he drove inside where he's even more dangerous."

All of this the pros realized. Tom Heinsohn, the coach of the Boston Celtics of the National Basketball League, said, "In our rating system, the highest number is five. Thompson gets 10 on his shooting alone."

Heinsohn would have loved to see David play for Boston but the draft rights to him went to Atlanta of the NBA and Denver. Each team was willing to meet his demands for a $3 million, six-year contract and it came down to a matter of where David wanted to play as a pro. He shocked the NBA by choosing Denver.

Thompson's attorney explained that David had thought about his decision for 10 days. He finally chose Denver because he thought he would be more comfortable there. David knew some of the Nuggets' players personally, particularly Bobby Jones of North Carolina and Towe, David's teammate at State. David also was impressed by Denver coach Larry Brown and by the fact that the Nuggets were a young team.

"I should fit right in," said David. "And I feel better about going into a situation where I won't be expected to completely turn a team around. Denver had the best record in pro basketball last year."

Indeed, Denver did have the best record, a 65-19 mark. But in order to get the draft rights to Thompson from Virginia, the Nuggets traded away All-Star players Mack Calvin and Mike Green and a top reserve, Jan van Breda Kolff. Rarely will a team value a rookie enough to get rid of two proven players, but David has more than lived up to Denver's expectations.

The Nuggets led the ABA in scoring average in 1975-1976, 121.87 per game, and again the team had the best record in either league with Thompson the star of the show. Only New York's Julius Erving and Indiana's Billy Knight topped him in scoring.

30

NETS
23

David accomplished all this while being the smallest forward in pro basketball in years. In the 1950's then-Boston-coach Red Auerbach shocked the NBA by making a forward out of 6-foot, 3-inch Frank Ramsey, an All-American from Kentucky. Ramsey was the first of the "quick" forwards.

Beginning with the 1976-1977 season, NBA teams had to cope with the very quick Thompson. His performance, though, would come as no shock. His ability had already been demonstrated.

None of the hoopla that has surrounded David since he first began to make headlines has seemed to change him. "My parents have done a lot for me," David says, "and I want them to be comfortable. I'm willing to provide any extravagances they want." David's dad, Vellie, a $6,000 a year janitor, couldn't be happier about that, and he has recalled how it all started.

"As he grew up," Vellie has said, "I could tell he was going to be different from the rest of us — he had talent. He used to sing so well in the church choir that people used to pay to hear him, that's how good he was. The other children, three boys and seven girls, they all did farm work. It was hard work, mostly picking cotton, but David was the baby, so he got out of it."

"By the time he was five, we sent him to school. He was big enough and there was no place else to leave him when we went to work. And Lordy, I remember that basketball. He used to do that more than anything. I remember how he used to turn on the car's headlights and play in the dark. I had to whup him for that every now and then to keep him straight."

Vellie even remembered when the game wasn't much fun for David, when he came home from ninth-grade practice one day in tears. "He said, 'Daddy, the boys at school say I hog the ball too much and I score too many points and get too many rebounds. They told me I was too greedy. What do I do?' " the elder Thompson recalled.

"I told him to score as many baskets as he could. When people say something like that, it means you must be doing something good, something nobody else can do. And that's when I realized maybe there was something in his basketball."

It didn't take long for the rest of the basketball world to realize it too.

GEORGE McGINNIS

Splashed around the Philadelphia landscape in the fall of 1975 were signs boasting, "By George, We've Got It" and "Let George Do It." With the bicentennial drawing near, a tourist might have thought the reference was to George Washington.

Fans of the Philadelphia 76ers, however, knew George Washington had nothing to do with the signs. Their George was McGinnis, a 6-foot, 8-inch, 245-pound forward who was expected to be the salvation of the team at the age of 25.

Their hopes were not without foundation. McGinnis led Philadelphia into the 1976 play-offs, the first time in years the 76ers had made the play-offs. The model of the power forward — McGinnis was big, strong, able to drive to the basket, and capable of rebounding with taller centers.

McGinnis even helped the 76ers to a brief stay in first place in the Atlantic Division of the National Basketball Association early in the season.

30

30

All this was with a team that just three years before had suffered through an 82-game schedule with only nine victories, the worst record ever in the NBA.

McGinnis, who earned the nicknames "Baby Bull" or "Big Mac" because of his size, was not the only reason for the turnaround, but he was the major one.

There had been a lot of reasons to believe that McGinnis would be able to accomplish a turnaround. For one, at an age when most players are just beginning to approach their potential, McGinnis was already an established star. He had already played four seasons for the Indiana Pacers in the American Basketball Association and, with Julius Erving, had been the most dominant player in the ABA.

The year before joining Philadelphia, George had led Indiana in every statistical category worth mentioning — scoring (29.8 average), rebounding (14.3), assists (6.3), steals (2.6), three-point percentage (.354). He also shared the league's Most Valuable Player award with Erving.

Before leaving Indiana, George had been the star of a home-town-boy-makes-good story that even Hollywood would have trouble believing.

McGinnis was born in Indianapolis and learned the game on the city's playgrounds. It was not, however, the only sport at which George excelled. He was also a standout in football at Indianapolis Washington High School — so good that 300 colleges recruited him.

But if George was good on the football field, he was devastating on the basketball court. In his senior year, he averaged 32.5 points per game — breaking retired pro superstar Oscar Robertson's Indianapolis high school record — and led Washington to a 31-0 record and the state championship.

Then tragedy struck the McGinnis family, always a close-knit group. That summer, while George was busy weighing the countless scholarship offers he received, his father Burnie, a 42-year-old carpenter, fell to his death from an eight-story scaffold.

"My dad and I were buddies," George has said, "but he'd beat on you if you did something wrong. When you succeeded at something, though, he was quick to praise. When my sister called me and told me my father fell, I suddenly didn't feel like going to college anymore."

George's mother, Willie, went to work on her son and by the end of the summer, she had persuaded him to attend Indiana. As a sophomore during his first varsity season (freshmen were not eligible then) George tore the Big Ten apart. He led the league in both scoring and rebounding, establishing a single-season point mark for the Hoosiers with 719 points, a 29.9 average.

That was enough for George. He knew he could play in the pros and talk of a merger between the two pro leagues worried him. He was afraid that salaries would fall if the ABA merged with the NBA which did take place after the 1975-1976 season.

McGinnis applied for the pro draft under the "hardship rule," something the pro basketball leagues devised to get around their own rule against signing players who had not completed their college careers.

George weighed his offers. They even included one from the Dallas Cowboys of the National Football League, who wanted him to play tight end, the position he played in high school. But George decided to stay at home and signed with the Indiana Pacers, who played in Indianapolis.

George proved his worth immediately. He averaged 9.1 rebounds and 16.9 points per game that first season, despite playing against much older players. He grabbed 400 more rebounds and scored 1,000 more points in his second year than he did as a rookie and has maintained that pace.

During his third season in the pros, George had started thinking about the NBA and had begun negotiations with that league. He played another year — 1974-1975 — for Indiana. Then came a tangled contract dispute in which George signed three separate multi-million dollar contracts with three separate teams — the New York Knicks, Philadelphia, and Indiana. He finally landed with the 76ers.

George doesn't apologize for the six-year, $3.2 million contract he received. "Let's be realistic," he once said. "One, I've only had two years of college education. Two, I'm black. And three, I'm not very smart, although I have a lot of common sense.

"My time is now . . . I don't see what's so complicated. Here's one pile of money and there's another. One pile is larger. It doesn't take any intelligence to figure that out."

30
FOX
35

30

George also is enjoying the challenge of the NBA. "In the ABA," he has said, "I could take a night off once in a while against teams like Memphis, Virginia, and San Diego; not that I could loaf, but I knew I didn't have to play quite as hard. But here, I have to bust my gut every night . . . I've looked at new teams and new players. They've helped my game. They've helped me extract all my ability."

There is a tremendous amount of ability to extract, too, and the 76ers realize it. For that reason, George is allowed to have far more freedom than the normal forward, who usually plays one of the corners.

If George wants to shoot from 25 feet, he does; if he wants to bring the ball down court, as he often does, he does that, too. George can run the offense from where a guard normally operates or drive to the basket when he wants. He presents more problems defensively than perhaps any forward in the game.

John Gianelli of the Knicks spoke about those problems after guarding McGinnis in one game. "I admit I gave him the outside shot," Gianelli told reporters. "He's a streak shooter and he wasn't shooting that well most of the time, so I just took a couple of steps back and let him fire. But I'll tell you one thing, he keeps coming at you. He asks for it (the ball) every time down the court."

Bill Sharman, the coach of the Los Angeles Lakers, once put it another way. "He's a 6-foot, 8-inch, 245-pound Earl Monroe," Sharman said, referring to the Knicks flashy guard.

McGinnis, himself, had a better explanation. "I think it's the inner drive in me to excel," he says. "I really enjoy competition."

The merger of McGinnis' former Indiana team, the New York Nets, David Thompson's Nuggets, and the San Antonio Spurs into the NBA for the 1976-1977 season also led to a startling player switch as the new season began. The 76ers acquired Julius Erving from the Nets. McGinnis and the Doctor, the shining lights of the now dead ABA, were suddenly teammates. The 76ers were immediately labeled title favorites.

As for the future, McGinnis has ideas about that, too. "I'd like to work with little kids, coaching," he has said. "There's entirely too much emphasis put on winning in this country. I've always done well under pressure, but I think it's a shame to make little kids play under it so soon."

JOHN HAVLICEK

John Havlicek is the Boston Celtics' version of the perpetual motion machine. He finally began to slow down in his 14th season in the National Basketball Association, but he was an important part of the Celtics' march to the 1976 NBA play-off championship.

The Celtics' forward was still always a step ahead of everyone else as the championship series carried into June. Slowing down only proved that he was mortal, a fact Boston foes had questioned through the years.

That the former Ohio State star was playing at all at the age of 35 was remarkable in itself. He never has had the physical attributes of the other stars of his era. A slim 6-foot, 5-inch, 215-pounder, Havlicek has played at a position that is dominated by larger, stronger men.

CELTICS
17

CELTICS
17

However, instead of letting his size hinder him, Havlicek made it work for him. He combined his natural quickness with unending hustle. He learned the game down to the tiniest detail. He concentrated on fundamentals. Havlicek therefore made it almost impossible for a bigger man to keep up with him when he was in his prime years.

If a big man tried to guard him closely outside, John would use his quickness to drive around him. That might leave a lane open to the basket. If not, it forced another opponent to pick up Havlicek, a move which would leave a Celtic teammate open for a pass. The result was the same, an easy two points.

Should a big man give him room to shoot outside and protect against the drive, Havlicek would score over him with 20-foot jump shots.

On defense, Havlicek relied on his quickness, his positioning, and his knowledge of how to cut off the passing lanes to become one of the best defenders in the game.

John also made use of his versatility to help the Celtics' attack. He is one of the few players in the game who is equally adept at two positions, forward and guard. As his body began to show signs of wear in 1976, he said that he actually preferred playing at guard because it was a position at which he was less likely to be injured.

But of all Havlicek's skills, perhaps the most notable is his ability to play as a member of the team. The game of basketball is a five-man game and the best teams have always had players whose talents meshed like the working parts of a fine watch. The Celtics have always emphasized the team aspect of the game and Havlicek was the main cog for many years. Sportswriters said the 1976 Celtics were "admittedly not a great team." But working together, they were champions.

Team play has brought the Celtics 13 NBA championships and Havlicek was a key in winning 8 of them. Since he joined the team in the 1962-1963 season, Havlicek has averaged 21.7 points and almost seven rebounds per game. His lowest point average was 14.3 in his rookie year when he was Boston's top reserve; his highest average 28.9 came in the 1970-1971 season. He has been a model of consistency.

During the 1973-1974 season, there was little argument that Havlicek was not only the best "quick" forward in the game, but also its best overall player. With Paul Silas operating as Boston's "power" forward on the other side, and the ferocious Dave Cowens at center, the Celtics had the best front line in basketball.

CELTICS
17

Havlicek played so well that he was named the most valuable player of the play-offs and the Celtics played their best as a team in five years. The result — Boston's first title since the 1968-1969 season.

Former Boston coach and now general manager of the Celtics, Red Auerbach, said then that "John Havlicek is what I always thought a Celtic should be. He takes charge in a quiet, unobtrusive way. I didn't think we'd be able to fill Bill Russell's shoes when the big man left, but of course John has."

Havlicek has carried that take-charge philosophy into his declining years. "The Celtics have always had an older person to try to pass along some of the team philosophy," he has said. "I've learned to fill that role to a certain extent."

Others in the league recognized in later years that Havlicek had slowed down, but their respect for him did not diminish. Larry Siegfried, a former teammate at Ohio State and with the Celtics, noted the change.

"He's using his head more now rather than the brute speed he used to rely on," Siegfried observed. "John doesn't have to work as hard as before, but when he has to, he does. John hustles; he still runs on the fast break. He still hits the open man with a pass, and, you know, whenever the Celtics need a big shot, guess who's gonna get the basketball?"

George McGinnis, the young, talented forward for Philadelphia, sees the same abilities. "Basketball is really played on knowledge," McGinnis once said. "The guy who knows more what he's doing can play it a lot easier than the guy with great talent who doesn't know how to play it. I don't think that John Havlicek is as extraordinarily talented as Dr. J, but Havlicek is just great. He uses his knowledge. He won't beat himself."

Havlicek is still the best middle man on the most successful 3-on-2 fast break in basketball and still one of the team's best playmakers. Though in 1976 he did notice the difference age caused, mostly on offense.

"I don't get the shot I used to get because I don't have the quickness or jumping ability," he commented. "Also I'm not being counted on to take quite as many shots as before. If I haven't got the good shot, I give the ball away. We have other guys able to shoot."

Though Havlicek began shooting less during the 1975-1976 season, the shots he was taking were better. He tried to shoot only when he could be squared away to the basket. As a result his percentage of shots made (about 47 percent) was the highest of his career.

Havlicek raised his play-off scoring total to 3,611 points in 1976. This makes him the third leading scorer in NBA play-off history.

Because he has always relied on basics, he noticed no drop off in his defensive ability. "I've always played fundamental defense," he says, "and I don't feel I'm getting beat in any certain way."

If all of that sounds as though Havlicek were ready for an old folks home, the reverse is true. An example of what the Celtics are like without him in the lineup illustrated that.

Early in March 1976, he suffered a knee injury which kept him out of six games. During his absence, the usually high-scoring Celtic attack did not once score more than 100 points. The team's five other forwards averaged a combined total of only 24 points per game.

Though slowed and bothered by his knee injury, Havlicek was still not thinking of retiring. His ambition was to become a 15-year man, something only two other players — Dolph Schayes and Lenny Wilkens — were able to accomplish. Even the thought of surgery did not cause him any fear.

"The rehabilitation aspect doesn't discourage me," he told reporters. "I have a lot of self-discipline and I'd punish myself to get ready. But if I went to training camp and found out I couldn't do it, I'd just hang 'em up. But at least I'd be able to say I gave it my best shot."

That's something John Havlicek has always given.

CELTICS
11
CELTICS

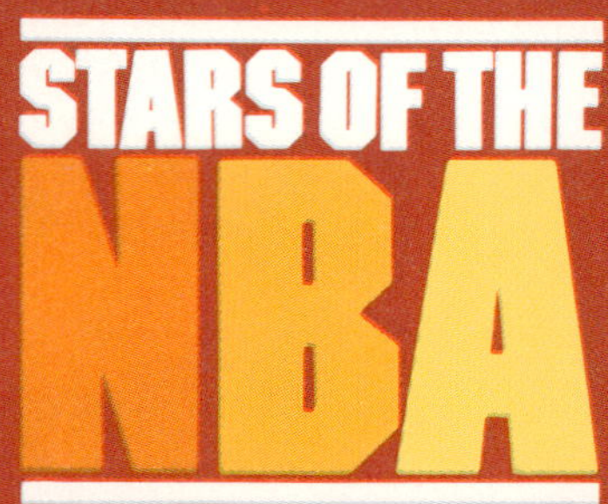

THE GUARDS
THE COACHES
THE CENTERS
THE FORWARDS